VISADAYOGA

(A Collection of Odia Poems in English)

VISADAYOGA

(A Collection of Odia Poems in English)

Phani Mohanty

Translated by
Aswini Kumar Mishra

BLACK EAGLE BOOKS
Dublin, USA | BBSR, India

Black Eagle Books
USA address:
7464 Wisdom Lane
Dublin, OH 43016

India address:
E/312, Trident Galaxy, Kalinga Nagar,
Bhubaneswar-751003, Odisha, India

E-mail: info@blackeaglebooks.org
Website: www.blackeaglebooks.org

First International Edition Published by
Black Eagle Books, 2022

VISADAYOGA
by **Phani Mohanty**
Translated by **Aswini Kumar Mishra**

Original Copyright © Phani Mohanty
Translation Copyright © Aswini Kumar Mishra

All rights reserved. No part of this publication may be reproduced, stored in a retrieval system, or transmitted, in any form or by any means, electronic, mechanical, photocopying, recording or otherwise without the prior permission of the publisher.

Cover & Interior Design: Ezy's Publication

ISBN- 978-1-64560-307-8 (Paperback)
Library of Congress Control Number: 2022947999

Printed in the United States of America

Dedicated to:

Adheep (Shubh)
my dearest grandson
who delivers me to his
priceless attraction
- **Aswini**

Preface

The title of this poetry anthology *Visadayoga* needs a reference to The Bhagabat Gita to make it less dizzyingly obscure for the English readers. In religiosity, the civilizational magnitude of India is rightly centred on Gita, for its logarithmic scale of brightness to enlighten a human soul. It borrows thoughts from Mahabharata, the Indian epic by Vyasadev. *Visadayoga* or the yoga of sadness robs Arjuna the zeal to fight on seeing the loved ones all around in Kurukshetra. Being disappointed he becomes pursuant to his argument before Lord Krishna not to fight. In reply, the latter advises his friend to fight in order that the cause of righteousness be ensured. 'If you give up this fight, you can't prove yourself the follower of a sinless path that would allow your reputation to lose' says he. This dilemma captures my poetic sense to concentrate in my metaphysical curiosity.

Coerced into the mundane world is perhaps my inevitable fate that can't be surmounted for the rest part of my life. Whatever one may struggle, he can't unyoke himself from the shackles to lead the life of sacrifice thus engaging fully with the halo around creativity. Unless one relieves himself from the fetters, initiative to celebrate the festival of freedom is a foregone conclusion. Such an enticement is the root of all sorrows, may be mundane or celestial. It is an impossibility for man to uphold the figuline picture of absolute freedom and integrity as long as he mortgages himself with external conditions. It is also an intractable affair to become the worshipper of beauty.

    The whole of the world is a barricaded prison for the detainees. The man is alive there as if under house arrest. It is a perpetual struggle for the man to escape from such a captivity wherein defeat is an assured winning wreath. Even though he knows well that ups and downs are not the characteristics of the soul but of the conscience, still regarding his soulful acquaintance, the inexperienced being has gained an idea since birth that he is singularly happy and unhappy both. He is destined for his helpless existence that stands at the central point of voluptuousness and disavowal. He has absolute ownership in the deeds earned from his previous birth. But he himself has no birth or death or idea as regard aftermath of the death. There too remains no possibility of the frequency of birth once a body is extinct. There has been no adequate understanding of ups and downs, happiness and misery. Still the half-witted human presumes the reflection as a real one rushing through moaning and despair. He is too jubilant with avarice, honeyed voice being allured to hedonism. Such an attachment gives rise to relationship. Moreover mutual attachment is the reason behind all bonding. Man forgets this, becomes frolicsome and aspires for ephemeral pleasure. Once this is over, it is inevitable on his part to return, this doesn't recur to his mind. Devoid of anxiety, ardour, fondness or indifference a life beyond all these is weak, gloomy and incapable to distinguish between good and bad. So long a man is deeply engrossed in his body-based mind, it is cumbersome to decipher the actual meaning of the facets of *Brahma*. In all ages and times, a man hypnotised by his senses suffers from plights. His existing life and afterwards are ruined. For hundreds of years, man being accursed, there has been no end to his Epicureanism. Words such as conscience, denouncement tend to become futile before him.

In our unknowingness, we try hard to flee away from the fetters of mundaneness but we hardly have time to know about its futility. Every struggling human being is like an animal laden with bags. The ageing ancient world spread about us is filled with concocted tales in every inch of its body. But we hardly have time for them. Like a lizard it is our blind fate to slither across the complex canvas of this universe. Since time immemorial, a routine life measured and captured accidently in our clenched fist is deceitful, tragic and lamentably loud. We lack discerning this much even. Due to our ignorance, incapability and abortiveness, being perplexed in a rueful condition we are forced to depend on the desired strength of an unimaginative formidable power. This compulsive cruel rule start assailing upon our ego and deeper self-confidence. Beneath the boundless blue sky in the measured and soundless disquiet life drama each one of us is a masked mechanical hero beating in void. Our grief is in corollary with that of Kurukshetra's Arjuna, lonely and nonplussed.

Arjuna's void and aloneness is over all not of his. In *Visadayoga*, he is not helpless or clueless. His tragedy is momentary and not everlasting. He was totally unsure of its depth. The crisis of Arjuna was not exclusively of him but of Krishna's too. Krishna was the cohort of Arjuna, intimate and trusted charioteer sticking together through thick and thin. Arjuna was always shocked with the pose of assured fearlessness. He was the successful partner of Krishna.

In Arjuna's body, breath and soul it was Krishna always. Endowed with the thought of Krishna, what was Arjuna's grief all about? What tragic one's or crisis! The mortal being of Arjuna was gratified due to the unconditional coverage of the time.

So Krishna was all along like a shadow in the company of Arjuna to redeem the latter from all crises. They were resolved in a simple and dignified way let alone impending sorrows and sufferings. Krishna is thankful to dispel attachment and grief both from the mind of Arjuna. Here, credit doesn't go to Arjuna. Krishna was the means to remove all tragic thoughts from him. Had Krishna absented himself from the war field, it was natural for Arjuna to embrace his fate like a common being. As a result, history would have been forced to take a different turn. Arjuna wouldn't have worn the Crest of Glory. He was like a puppet at the command, advice and rule of Krishna. In the whole of his life Arjuna became a toy whose key was with Krishna. Therefore in *Mahabharata* Arjuna is exceptional. He could say with pride: 'for aeons, I am merged with the root of your body hair'.

Arriving at the last decade of the century, a man of our times on the eve of a new unknown century faces a didactic tussle thus spending days in crisis. He doesn't know how to resolve it. There is not a single selfless like Krishna displaying brotherhood to save us from an appalling situation. Within and outside there have been incessant rains of restlessness decked with hollowness. His mortal life is smothered and devastated like a worn out stick. Man is bound to live within that irksome life circle devoid of any definite radius. The pitiable existence of a human being is like a disfigured cardboard but to lead a meaningful life how futile are our attempts and desires in extreme. Like other people of our generation I am unwanted so much before the sizeable physique of time. Many secret pains of untold atrocities have unanimously been burdened by the luck on me. I am bruised and wearied by the combined injustice of fate and man. I have faith no more on me like before. I can't whip on my disobedient, unrestrained, unstable and untiring mind. I am impatient due to my inherent helplessness. Like the sky, I am all along without a friend. There is not a single kin in this shattered and grief-stricken life. It is not my fate being hatred, scolded, defamed, overlooked and disliked. My contradictory set up is strengthened from time to time. Ideologue and dignity are extinct. It is accidental like breaking the summit of a mountain. I am protagonist of the episodes shrouded in mystery. I pray, the sorrows and tragedies as I undergo shouldn't at all happen to others.

I am not indebted to anyone including fate and God. My obstinate and one-sided mind is not controlled by any external conditions. I don't have a mind that makes a life meaningful. I feel always, as if I am encountering a cyclone that would blow out my thatched world smashing my existence. Had I been aware to cope with my environment, I wouldn't have suffered like a capsized boat. Amid adversity without aspiring to achieve anything I run forward with a mind, transfixed. From asceticism to worldly life, it is long cherished. I am mad after the dream of an ominous, cursed life. I am the silent uproar and wordless echo of my life. I am also silent and absorbed totally in my unbending solitude.

Life is not only attractive muscles. Bone marrow too is a significant part of life. One day each part of my body may come to the use of someone, although inevitably the blood and flesh would rot and mix with the soil. One day or other this rotten body would do away with this world. Death is a must, nevertheless the infatuated mind is mad after creativity and this is beyond my comprehension. Of course a selfish honest man, even if conscious of his pride, he struggles always hopefully to lead a dignified life. Whereas he burns like a flicker of light for the whole of life and death in the hand of an unknown, unfamiliar and invisible one.

I know my limited and contracted ability. In a life of woe and misery, there is none to be called as kin and wouldn't too. In the middle of my life, those I had accepted selflessly as kin, they are now slipping away one after another from the map of my mind. Unfortunately some have become my dearest enemies. Looking at my defeat they now celebrate their victory blowing a conch shell.

The extreme betrayal of kin proves more excruciating for me than passing. Life proves lonely and fruitless like the pitiable long breath of a deplorable candle. I am bathing in the tears of Ganga defying the fear of attack and failure. In order to expiate for the same I celebrate mourning with sincerity. Those who raised my hands with love have ripped apart them with the envy and selfishness of a *kirpan*. Their handwriting would remain in golden letters in the forehead of the ever dancing time. God would never forgive those deceptive men for such a moral breakdown.

Today such peculiar interrogations spring up in my mind to which I don't have any satisfactory answers. Although the whole of life was tormented with many things, what did I gain out of it? Do vocabularies like blame, defame, rebuke, hatred envy are justified for a wholesome dedicated life. All along since olden times death has been keeping a vigil on me and my dearest foes but what a terrible desire in mind to lead a simple, peaceful and immaculate life.

What tiny beings we are before the eternal dimensions of the creation. Those who don't have a relationship with the ebb and flow of my life what of that to them on my death? Being afraid of death I am not that man to humiliate death. In which word or language, the pictorial scene of death can be described. The cry of the ominous air is always heard from my breath. Beneath the grey sky due to the untold repression of the domestic enemies the dusty face of man looks pale like a corpse. The sky and the space reverberate with the screaming of the vulture. No rule of law or social commitment persists, let alone the justification of birth right.

I am a momentary guest, burdened with loan to the maximum. When I would get rid of the curse, who knows? So much of care takes effect to *live* the life of a new one. As we love life there has been weakness in everyone's heart towards it. It is my continuous journey from one sphere of loneliness to another. Lying in the benighted corner of the devastating world like a dead rat, I brook all illegality, atrocity and injustice.

It matters little for the time whether I am here or not. My disobedient impassable mind is like a faltering leaf in the air. I am impatient due to my inherent helplessness. At each moment the shadow of my inexpressible fear devours me like a Rahu. I await like the owner of a destroyed field lest there would be someone to reach and look at me at once and pat me affectionately from head to toe.

As I have listened to, melancholia doesn't assail upon a body if a man is healthy. It too doesn't lay hold of a good person. I am neither of the two. Hence, like a shadow, I am sure to be gripped by desolation for all time to come. I have no escape from the bestial clutch of it. It would discharge its duty like an intimate friend until my last breath. I would bid adieu to it smilingly thus lying over its lap. The upcoming century would consider, if I have kept my promise or not. If not during my life time one day or other, a mighty man endowed with moral health would tear apart history to take birth on earth. He would change the current trend of history to become an ideal of its flow.

Before closing my eyes and before I turn into lifeless, I would politely make a small request to my loving known and unknown readers, let alone my self-centred children and envious kin.

'I entreat, after my passing, no one should take pity on me. Don't send any condolences to my grief stricken family. Don't print a word in any newspapers, no meeting of any sort. Don't perform or celebrate any obsequies or birth anniversary. Immerse all my unpublished manuscripts along with my ashes. Don't tell anyone that the poet of *Visadayoga* was a talented one of seventh decade.

If the above request could be kept, then my soul would rest in peace in the after world. It is sheer foolishness to bestow mercy or compassion for a dead one. One should pave way for him silently.

Silence is my greatest gift to this life. I have no avarice for fame, respect, pleasure, property, gift or jewellery. I have no ambition or weakness. The posterity shouldn't be inspired with my peculiar ideals. As I have decided to tread on the dark path, they, even mistakenly shouldn't step on it. The setting sun shouldn't be their ideal. They should live banking on their strong self-reliance and scribble history of the new century with a new language.

Phani Mohanty

Translator's Note

This is the first full-fledged English translation of Odia poet Phani Mohanty's *Visadayoga* incorporating 38 poems published in 1992.

His poems would be better if they reach prospective international readers through translations and help shaping a concrete idea on Asian writing focussing India, which naturally rolls down to Odisha. Of late many places in the world have truly become multilingual and multicultural espousing a purpose of this kind. This collection is a tenor to hold on Bhagavad Gita, the philosophy contained therein ascribing melancholy which is till now inaccessible to many. Here, many of the poems are in tune with the same having distinctive originality of their own. The poet is absorbed into the cultural milieu of the Odia race perceptively examining his creativity through it. In his poems the culture specific terms and symbols are close-packed and therefore it became strenuous for me to carry them exactly into an alien language like English. The rhythmical structure vis a vis music of the poems are no less. Prabhat Nalini Das in her English translation of the Odia fiction *Amrutara Santana* by Gopinath Mohanty has observed:

> 'It is a part, and often, a very important part of the culture that the language represents. The greater the component of the imaginative and creative language

used in a given work the greater the difficulty in rendering it in another language'

However, I have tried in my own capacity to bring both the languages to a common wave-length to resolve the untranslatable characteristic of the incomprehensible lines in some poems. At times I have no other means than to put the original Odia word with a foot note for better understanding of the readers.

To me the poet is essentially a poet of the east. Therefore his poems are not adorned with western thoughts or ideas. They do not follow a common pattern to become sentimental but the intricacies of thoughts fall easily into a phase of native consciousness rejecting many things as exotic. Theological lexicons are his all-time favourites. Spiritual beliefs find way to his creative impulse and they act like lens to discover the civilizational set up of Odisha. The rhythmic structure in his poems arranges words pleasant to the ears. The undertone is sonorous. The quality of his poetic output is basically a compression to the design of his divine psyche. I, as a translator can't but compromise with the intellectual godliness of the poet's creativity. I wait for a different occasion to express my own views as regard the poetic synthesis since my role is limited here discharging the responsibility of a translator only.

However, we have a common motto to glorify the magnificence of poetry and invite all including readers of this book to identify with its magnetic vastness. This is also an opportunity for me to join with you all to celebrate the poetical aspect of our living.

Aswini Kumar Mishra

Contents

Preface	7
Translator's note	15
From cradle to the grave	19
Each life	23
Attraction, so much	24
Beyond my intellect	26
At whose unreached destiny's	28
All my evanescent memory	30
I am the trusted slave of my	32
This life, devoid of solace and support	34
What a frantic, heart-rending eagerness	36
At each moment	38
Love of a poet	40
Unknown, who is my	42
Each of my moment	43
Half of my life is perished	45

Whatever new style the life	47
I, myself a slanderous hero	49
The festival of Visadayoga	50
My holy native land	52
Life all through with ambition	54
What a tragic irony	57
I am tired, exhausted too much	60
Whichever manner I wish to speak	62
My fate, most unfortunate	63
Where is the incentive to cross over?	65
If at all death has to arrive	68
In every blink, like the dark clouds	70
In my hand, the lethal pot	72
One day or other	74
In the turning point of history	76
What do I feel like this at times?	78
I know doubly	80
For whom this mourning	82
It is my misfortune that	84
The pathway of this world is	86
One day or other	88
In my bewail and tear	90
Come. Oh! Revered guest	91
The time of your arrival	92

One

From cradle to the grave,
life in its entirety
is full of tribulations.
Times, nowhere watertight
like past, present or future
no beginning or end
no word to denote
each bereft of meaning
in a world, undeluded.
Wherever one gazes upon
the dense foliage of singleness,
mind, widowed
cruel derision of divinity
in the space aloft
whirling vanity of *mayachakra*[1]
gala of festive scenes
its exact apparition can't be
delineated by any
in this mundane world.
How small I am of that
awful scene
my gross physique
made of *panchabhuta*[2]
seeing Him overwhelmed
so much, my whole being turns fatigue, listless
and my warring spirit disappears.

---

1 Cosmic illusion unfolding waves and particles through mental awareness
2 Esoteric combination of earth, fire, air, space and water

I forget at once
my indomitable valour
virility, grandeur of a workful life
my intense
intellectual and religious avowedness
for aeons, I keep quiet
like a forbearing Earth
with least agreement
or controversy.
As a part of that
visible and invisible universe
great and kind hearted
like the delicate touch of the trope of *Bibhuti*[3],
a little of the undiminished
unapparent existence,
mundane, I surrender to a life in penury, much scattered,
eclipsed with enthralment of
pleasure and sorrow.
I am not that fortunate
to equalise with that reckless
unimaginable spirit,
like an aspirant
to encounter with outcry
of the opposite
or to transcend a mortal life
wearing His virtuous titles
like a festoon.

---

3   The sacred powder

Like a seer, even if
I spend life in the manner whatever,
I don't have any redemption
no salvation in this world, impetus
no escape from His fuming and
ravenous look, from His burning appetite
frequent changing hues of the
wide open mouth and its scary abyss
its hypnotic labyrinth of illusion, ever whirling
wheel of time
the *chakrabyuha*[4]
Each man's fate is that of Arjuna's
every poet, too similar to
that of him
nothing like past, future or present
neither beginning nor end
nor shackle nor freedom
the whole cycle of living, passing
is filled with tragedy.

---

4   The intricacy of a war design made against enemies by Kaurav in *Mahabharat* to kill Abhimanyu son of Arjuna from Pandav group.

Two

Each life
epitomises grief and pity
from cradle to the grave
spectres of fear and terror
stifle the mind.

Neither hope nor expectation
no relief from the clutches
of life and death,
no chance of gaining
any rare wealth in life
no word sprouts
to claim life or earth
as of my own.

This body, dark complexioned
bends down before age and disease
tired and indifferent
from head to toe
fear, unknown grips me
breathless for the pain
intolerable and mind in haste
disorderly, event turns mishap
the wobbly black cobra
bites and the spot turns blue
oozing blood.

My helpless extant
is like a man unwanted
in the dreadful womb of eternity
despite cruel and brutal expression,

death dances in my front
as destined for the man's fate
succumbs to attachment.

His heartrending sanguine history
philosophy of life stand ephemeral,
fortune, barbaric
I am at the crossroads of Trishanku[5]
devoid of prosperity
static, motionless
before the despotic rule
nowhere, the way out.

What an irrepressible existence
miserable plight! Alas!! Undone
never a question of willing, unwilling
know not caste, race, colour or character
whom were I born to?
have no strength to utter
the same candidly.
I am an explosion
Unsolicited and accidental

born out of the blazing fire
of clandestine love
sensual and unworldly
scoffing daily about
jungle of Arjuna[6]
overlook always
like an eerie and hazy life

---

5   A legendary king, creator of a middle sky between heaven and earth
6   A tree famous for its herbal status

Three

Attraction , so much
for the discourse
of this dismal life
frailty too, as I survive
and continue yet
hours, months and annums
no scope of being unyoked,
the script of my cruel
fate is full of adventures
spread over centuries.

Still, no respite
from the pattern's wheel
of the tragic and tempting life
the methodical soul and body tuck into desires
overcome by pangs and worries,
listless, rust and indifferent
the endless eternity
jeers at me in the
consecrated fire of life.

Destined to born
I am muffled, fall off and a toy
in the hands of the almighty
who's fabulous Bibhuti
regulates water, sky, earth and the space
leave aside the sun, moon, planets
and stars, thirty three crore
are the pliant deities
a deep embrace of compassion
and love have made me

blind and ignorant
its rhythmic balancing fall
has reverberated the golden India.
I don't aspire to a throne
or a mat studded with gems
no need for sunshine, vigour
or a quiver for Gandiv[7]
no need for strength or kingdom
crown of gold, chariot or applause

On earth, my remains
are consigned to flames finally
I am tiniest, an entity of the
great pitiful abstract,
a searing pain within.

---

7   bow

Four

Beyond my intellect
and illusory aureole
lies the boundless orbit,
the infinite sleep of
kala-Bhairabi[8]
in the final cantos
of the reminiscence,

Dead is the conscience
and cognitive power, dreams knocked a gentle
and refined life out
future stands gloomy,
unlearned, knowledge restricted
and the gross body gifted from
the deity is moribund.

Where is my hard- earned
fortune? To rid of the circle of vision
spread across
the horizon and to lead a calm, austere
sinless life, to escape from desire, lust
and dip in the world of
pain and pleasure.

On the other
My compact world
Is resonated with disgrace,
beating of mind and heart,
wit and law thoughtless
human values meaningless

---

8   name of the goddes

policies and rules sinful
deceitful maxims of *prabajya*,⁹
pursuits occupying lust
I am that helpless fool
not being assigned duties.

---

9   To renounce the world and accept the life of an ascetic

Five

At whose unreached destiny's
unwritten command
a battle cry
ushers in by the domestic enemies
the honorific holy India
is bruised and scarred
by killing, depredation, arson
and ravishment.

In the age-based man's
voluntary *tandav* dance
his sharp-edged sword's
rattled rhythm, in the airy display
of illusory war
the mystery of eternal creation
is sanguine.

So trivial I am
don't have any aim or ideology
nothing to brag about
like a God, no effort
leave alone integrity
life, cursed
pain, uninterrupted
famously spread around the universe
transcending time
every moment scary
laid waste with fear, unknown.

A man, yet commonplace I am
with flesh and blood

of the visible universe
swamped with emotion and love.

My pretty world is
ransacked with fiery fury
of the destiny yet to manifest,
hissing of fear
noises very often
from my innermost body.

Six

All my evanescent memory
of bygone days, like a spear
pierces into my mind and body
night and day, life precious,
unsteady lotus heart
smells bitter, conscience bites
unlucky I am, without virility,
in every step of the ongoing society
my existence
doesn't get hold of,
unpresentable ever.

In my dreams, I do come across
a picture, uncommon whose limbs, soul,
conscience are evoked with announcement
of the holy chant covering
dovishness and compassion.
The lotus heart vibrates
time and again with the syllabic
'Om'. The grand meet of love and amity
embellishes each page.

India, the jungle of my dream,
saddles through killing, enmity, skirmish,
and the flagrance of Eros
they all shrink it.

In every bit of consciousness,
rhythm of heroic smartness repeats
along the futile directive of shouldering duty of
one's own

the whole extant
is obsessed with immorality
and non-ideals.
Where are people without
bewail? A safe abode, where is that?

Going back and forth
The shackles of natural law
The broadening smoke of endless Bibhuti
amidst, the world class
Gandiv[10] loses track
eyesight weak, pang and prick
all over the limbs
the body looks dismal
staging a scene, baleful.

---

10   The famous bow used by Arjuna in Mahabharat

Seven

I am the trusted slave of my
belligerent ego, conscience dismal
the soul smothers, uneasy grows
self-inflicting arousing queasiness
void of memory and.

The solitary self
wishes to escape from life but
how to get rid of the pangs of childhood
young and old days'
past, present and future
dawn, noon and evening
the three periods
spreading across the night
freedom is farsighted,
for years together
to lead the life of a lowly useless
without aims and ideals
with faltering limbs
and bustling anxiety,
thus mundane body
a part of moral revolt
is extinct aplenty in time.

A life shaded
and the rest forsaken
a futile redemption from the earth or heaven
allowing ignominy
to spread about.

What a labour!
Lassitude to acquire a quiet mind,
austerity with a flair for yoga
What a surprise!
I am that protagonist
discredited, defeated time and again
in the war with life,
the earth is frightened
due to my misdeeds
the water, earth and the sky
all are reverberated with
the victor's joy
and my ulterior ego
overshadowed my conscience.

Eight

This life, devoid of solace and support
singularly alone, an ephemeral guest I am
deep dark around, my *tapasya*
falls apart, unseen, quotidian futility
for an era and the universe.
Still no escape
from the round shaped
shackles of duty, no relief
from the mundane chains,
orbit of lust, no riddance from the fetters
of *Sattva, Rajah & Tamah*[11]
and the illusory encirclement
of the supreme consciousness
of the brightened spirit
acquired thereof.
What a strange mystery!
this one, always inevitable
no beginning or end
invisible, unuttered.

I am ,in the eternal frame
of eternity, a smallest being
cursed, unarmed, lost
with least trying, invisible cruelly
enveloping mystery.

No aim or attentiveness
not even a speck of focussing or self confidence
no easy or natural expiry

---

[11] The first stands for spiritual purity and the other two impurity

in this luscious world
no way than the self-willed expiry
nothing expedient.
Whereas a lorn psyche
of affliction and attachment
burning with the flaming desire
I am tired, overwhelmed
and burnt to ashes.

Nine

What a frantic, heart -rending eagerness
for all time freedom!
What a worry
to slip away from this mundane existence!

But what a cruel irony of fate,
smothered deeply with the paradox of
desire and lust.

I am the shameless protagonist
of an oral past, beguiled
by the occult of lexicons
petrified, untamed,
the body of Krishna's hue
defeated always by the
icy cool anguish
dreams forsaken.

This, the invisible fate
of each poet of our time,
one has to undergo the deeds
of one's own for centuries
no excuse or generosity
a life has shrunken with the weight of sin
transcends possibility of its
sudden decline,
no end of emotion or attraction
from the deity's curse.

The heart is restive
like a sea, devastating

the mind in disarray
full of struggles
life, mechanised and woeful
hazy, misty
the great eternity
is bemused with
the festival of destruction.
Earth, stricken with fear
by deceptive eve,
the jungle India of my dream
is rhymed typically
by its rise and fall.

Ten

At each moment
like a sullen Pandav
exhaling the flash of my conscience
I am unruffled, immobile
underwhelmed, discernment of life and death
everything fate-oriented.

From cradle to the grave
my life span
is sure and certain

In the ultimate year of the century
for which fame and laurel
the grand festival of crashing down
blaring, drumming
the three worlds
pulsate with a warring mood
the whole life is stifled by the
solid and uncontrolled arms.

The blue future
Tenses up and cracks apart.

Despite defeat and disappointment
one has to live on so long alive
with periodic rise and fall
ill fated even if
one has to aim his arrow
at the fish's eye
minutely.

One has to dissect the utopian world
the sinless honeyed grove of the
ignoble poet, his impeccable
utterance, fists clenched into
his might and inflated self-reliance.

What kind of justice, righteousness
of a behaviour this one?
Discipline either.
Since there is no other
World, one has to take to bits
The hard-earned emotions
saved through life,
the elusive love too.

Eleven

Love of a poet
remains a questionnaire always
for people of all ages
and beyond.

No answer yet
in the gold yielding blue India
even though depredated with
sin and unjust,
no way other,
no question arises to justify my
individual rights, height or ideal.

To me,
no dictionary is close at hand
in this visible world
to decipher the meaning
of each word, anything enjoyable
even acquired very hard
is pulled down before my very eyes
no way out of the same
for me.

I am only a part of the
cog and wheel of some
celestial power
unknown and strange
each of my extant is controlled
at the behest of some
unbeatable vicious orders
the dream of integral freedom
is far off, in this life

one has to undergo the result
of a previous birth
that one is destined for.
In sorrow and happiness
victory and defeat
I am unperturbed, unmoved
in humiliation and song of adulation.
Stable I am
and my heart thunder like
remains stout.

There is nothing like
dear or hated
still the unruly mind
is stirred and wobbly
at times suffused with exalted dreams
no words blow up, all along
life pulverises with a moaning
like a captive I am exiled within
stricken with fear
all the while.

Knocked out by untold penury
My fate is sealed
The world, honeyed
is filled with the enigma
of an illusory war,
incessant falling of night
from the blue-sky
the three worlds and periods
appear like a mirage
the worlds, both seen and unseen
play with the endless nothingness
in a void.

Twelve

Unknown, who is my
Lord, beneficiary?
Which one to enjoy
no way to ascertain,
when middle aged
the ignoble poet's fate
is sure to be ruined.

Maxims, so much,
sermons flawed, impoverished
and infidelity to protect righteousness
neighing of immoral and evilness
body and limbs
tired, fatigue and downhearted.
The self-centred, phony
swarm of locusts play *hori*[12]
with blood, burn torch
using my tears.

Like Draupadi, unclothed
how unsure I am
perplexed, coward ad frail
before me there has been
dance of death
all along, pose and gesture
espousing a shielding area
of protectiveness.

---

12   Festival of colour

Thirteen

Each of my moment
is pressed with
woe and anguish, my conscience
resonates with the discordant
music of death, unusual
that it has not the beginning or end,
my whole life, whole world
shiver down the spine
my virility, self worth
crush with time
to identify with the soil.

Like a craven
Every scene appears
hazy and pale before me
still my full-hearted ego
intermittently pounds
my soul like a harlot.

Had I known such an ill fate
have gone searching
pathway to life
in a hideous and bending pose,
in each case I wouldn't do to
distinguish between sin and virtue
moral and immoral
and had preferred to yoke
under the rule of law.
In a natural manner
being pressed with
to ensure good and bad

of the rest life,
like a committed one
would of fight alone in the war
between two charioteers.

For all time
my birth would have
shrouded in mystery,
there won't be any fear
for God or demon
in land, water, sky and fire.

Despite recurrent defeat
in the fiercely drawn warring life
my exalted life is engaged foolishly
day and night,
my wit, sensibility
too comply with the awful world.

My masculinity
roars in vain
everywhere from ghost to Yaksha
Naga to threadworm, moth to insect
even if defeated in each cell.

Fourteen

Half of my life is perished
in my mother's womb, the other half
shattered by the *karalachakra*[13] disc.
I am born bracketed with adversaries
and cruel minds, this rare birth
an accidental bring up, predestined
taking a snooze deeply
like an icing fish
coincidental so much.

In this mortal world'
life, synonym of the body
made of *panchabhuta*[14]
shackled by the
world is not the ultimate,
beyond this, innumerable imaginative worlds
unfathomed seen and unseen
since million of light year
enveloping shaded darkness layer after layer
and through the doors of a
flimsy dark tunnel
in the azure sky, air and space
staged like everyday copulation.

Such a frail body
of flesh and blood
ageing and death
of disease and lament
incapable to infer the meaning

---
13   dreatful wheel
14   five elements

of the obscure *Shastra*
ever confidential,
the other name of
the *panchabhuta*
is life.

Fifteen

Whatever new style the life
adapts to pass on
there is no escape from the great impassivity,
from the holy fire of life *yagna*
wooden yokes
and the inevitable flow of events.

There is no end to my ignorance
and helplessness
no possible way to get rid of the
collective pain.

It is the fate of each poet
to undergo the tiredness of defeat,
sorrows, infirmity, futile masculinity,
mocking of fate, the time ,insurmountable
and formidable it is the fate of each poet
to lay half dead with least controversy or condition
tapping into micro
bit of consciousness.

Time and again
In whatever way
the sky appears bright-coloured'
the ether makes much sound
the body engulfs in
sorrow and anguish
sorrow and anguish,
appalled by pleasure
and sacrifice
one has to conceal his head

between the knees and wait for ages
the dictate of fate until dissipation
of the known and unknown
visible, invisible
and clusters of the universe
followed by unveiling of the
unimaginative mystery
desisting oneself from the great
attraction and invisible shackle.

Time and again
from one breath to another
the space in between
burns away by
awe and fire.

Totally personal
stifled, lamentation
oozes out, one has to wait
for until being relieved fully of the
illusory world.

In the heaviness of sin
even if the cursed word is crumbled hugely
to the ground, an innocent life
vanishes into speechless silence
one has to pull on with
this mundane world singularly
dead like from century to century
encountering catastrophic regime of Manu.

Sixteen

I, myself a slanderous hero
of the past tales,
a wholesome man of the
incomplete love making
ramshackled by the fear of
disorder and concurrent pain.
Each of my artery, muscle, blood cell suffer
from an icy cold grief
body, ageing and diseased
shudders like a banyan leaf
life, as if a floating object
in the turbulent sea, astir.

The unflagging ego
indomitable sexual urge
amid the conflagration
of total catastrophe
and to become dispirited
is what life.

When there is no strength
to resist the opponent by body
made of five elements
the tall masculinity
lacks ability to solidly string the bow
no reprieve, compassion or bounty is there
layer wise, freezing like a massive land
spreading across its body
the immeasurable sea, forlorn
stretches far beyond.

Seventeen

The festival of *Visadayoga*,
without sound, colour
or look is acted upon far beyond
the horizons, encompassing the earth,
sky and the land of Nagas,
their photos smoky
visible ever through the
aureola and life, untiring
full of magical events
calm in life and death
unfaded.

Obsolete are the *shastras*
and *puranas* for a man of the mortal world
all aid and advice futile
from cradle to the grave
everywhere the
dreadful whip of rule.
Which age-long man's
curse is this? Scary deed of time's
secret command
scripting the fate of each poet.

The poet's sin
is the replica of his immaculate ego
his fate is the virtue of his
deep self-reliance,
the luck of a dissatisfied human.

The poet in his moribund state
Celebrates the merit of body and soul,

Like a *siddhayogi*[15]
sermonises 'everyone lives on his own'
there is no way out
from the accumulated pain
of *kapatapasha*[16]

The allurement of the
mundane world gets exhausted
before me since the auspicious
moment of my birth,
with the load of paradoxical thoughts
my soul, innocuous
gets tired intermittently.

---

15   An ascetic with self realisation
16   beautiful way of playing dice

Eighteen

My holy native land
suffers from grief, immeasurable
my country, unique in its strength
and great is the person within her.

In the wilderness of the
first touch, I forget doctrine of the
ancient religiosity and sermons
the poet detracts amid woman and gold
boasts overwhelmingly in vain.

For which curse of the person from
history, the lotus heart
is down with worries
no lust or pleasure, royal wealth
no cheers up for peace and non-violence
there is no end to hope and fear
no question for exercising one's right
day and night, each moment
month and year, alert and curious in
perpetual wonder,
a new world is reflected
with the billowing consciousness.

From one sunlit to the other
the poet is absorbed in unresisting love
drinking the nectar
atma-sudha-mruta.[17]

---

17   Ambrosia for the soul

Temperamentally in fearsome costume
armour made of bones
wreath of Rudraksha beads
on the chest, in every pore of the skin
the cupid arrow pierces , in the unspoken womb
of anguish, wintry cold,
the body and mind of the poet declines.

This being unique of an experience
filled with tremor
without repeat or end in any *shastra*
no tiredness in company or intimacy
no way to escape from the silken trap
the lonely, silent existence
is worried night and day
being the world afraid of.

In this life many stood untold,
in every birth and time, my life
made of *panchabhuta* would smother
in a wondrous way
the slander laugh falling out of the
closed lips at an unprepared moment
with ever surprisingness.

Nineteen

Life all through with ambition
and self-confidence, since ages
I wait for your return with unblinking eyes
and wounded ego,
like a dark cloud as if to rain over the deep blue circle
not a single word would come out
of the illustrious countenance,
not to deform the clay idol
with the bomb of an alphabet
should strive hard for a life
without tragedy
at the time bidding adieu.

Despite the combined injustice
of fate and man would try to find the way for an exit
may lose blood thereon,
the imaginative crime and
unfaithful, insurmountable
destiny would create bruises
around me all along
covering the whole of life and death.

Still I am not dead but alive
amid the devastating sea water
half-drowned
I wait for the new sun to welcome.
Since birth, I am well aware
I am a part of the instant
A moment's moment
A possibility's possibility
dream and desire of the early rain

I am a spark of the *mahakala*
a fallen meteor, for the springing toy
worthless evaluation of the
existence, resounding with words.

Questions after questions,
hundreds, quiver persistent
by the stinging of conscience
burnt, scarred
sanguine, a scorched life
like a wounded bird
in metaphysical grief
merged with oneself
doubtful is the mind and heart,
the entire life is terrified
like an unresolved fate
painful excruciatingly.

My cursed life
a father's progeniture
is made of different stock
my mind and sensibility are
in a fix
like a heartunable
to polarise between behaviour
and accent.

The invisible bondage
is shrouded in unknown mystery
both past and future
are shivered with
the spectre of ominosity.

A life, total escape from adversity
is an impossibility for the mortal world
the body and soul are regularly
pressed into
this life journey
the cruel destiny is yet to triumph over.

The region, boundless
bereft of light and happiness,
helpless is the existence
of a mortal being
day by day prone to decline.
bit by bit.

Where is that beautiful
Hale and hearty being filled
with happiness?
Where is the qualified greenness
of small time dream and hope?
source of light, a partial sloth
half awake, the proximity of soil.

To step ahead and again
to retreat a couple of steps
this only firm and certain
like a death line
and the slender humour
of an enigmatic God.

Twenty

What a tragic irony
the fate line has! The cruel blow
of an ambush strike in full knowledge
of the misfortune's evilness,
in this world
there is no truth other than
the relative truth amid the illusory halo
of the film of desire and lust.

No scope for self-development
no way seen for self-promotion
yet, no words have been scripted
taking the new edition of life.

Despite the lethal pain
this life is dreamy and colourful
longest exile of extreme failure
unknown though, in each vein and sinew
the naked rejoicing of the
wrestling demon.

The skin wrapped body of mine
is eclipsed by an eerie spirit,
like a bad planet, at every moment.

Each moment
catches my dismal mood
every night cold and immovable,
every point of exit
is closed and enigmatic.

Awareness and expression
earthly impulse
the proximity and touch of Bhabagata
so many directives, rules for the
intellectual world
post-human, the integral
fight between law and lawlessness
cruel rule, candid dismay and
the memory in delusion
amid mysterious self-realisation.

No effort to rise high
no fear or hold back
no envy towards any
nothing in fate like
sweetness, indescribable
my luck is pictured with
demean and satire
every life time is
saturated with death
each death, a disaster
like last step of the
final journey.

In the far off horizons, amid an unimaginative scene
the dark-hued cloud of rancour
envelopes evenly , death imminent
the indescribable silence, transfixed
curse of the deity, in fact
this is my fate.

you ten *Dikpals*[18]
pardon my ineptitude
my unnatural silence,
hollowed ego
my generosity may be reprieved, O God, inebriated
have my birth right
on duties only.
I am only a descendent of
that *karma*.

I am only a shadow of the time tree
pale and hazy
today I exist, tomorrow may not
centering on my continuity, many things would
take turn in the visible world
incidentally, amid the
blanched orbit of my vision

The mind and body
are the honeyed pot of eros
the burning inferno
old and death
plight and misery
would line up
with my fate.

In every death, the life-line
would lengthen,
the unyoked time would strive
recklessly
marching ahead.

---

18   ten gods in ten directions

Twenty one

I am tired, exhausted too much
it is not easy to erase my fate line
for me, the cure is rare and can't be found
so easily. Futility, defame,
rebuke and humiliation
shatter me mechanically.
My life, this is after all.

In the honeyed grove of time
formality is searched for,
the frolicsome childhood is
filled with blind parental love
my broken fate is treated with
the paste of red sandalwood
and angelic wreath, the brazen confession
of my own incapability
a futile step to console oneself
this has been my determined fate.

Still from vase to vase, scene to scene
from this world to the after world
making a bleeding quest, despite failure
narrowing the brooding sentiment
one has to walk down alone
shouting impassionedly.

I am never above words
nor their under
in the sense organ of a man
filled with words
I am in the middle point

of life and death
like an empty pot with triviality.

I am the mute witness of
a worldly expanse
the chain of affection
is loosened, the great decline
of sensual enjoyment
a preface to the
undiscovered, unforeseen
chapter.

'Again birth and death again'.
Life, just a condition
on the floating expanse of time
a pure life divided'
terrified all by the uncertain future
up to the definite present.

The eloquence becomes decrepit
connotes a different meaning of the
voicing strength, nowhere to
conjoin or deduct a word
the precious life is immersed
gradually with the eternal womb
day by day.

Twenty two

Whichever manner I wish to speak
still my thoughts stand
incomplete like the most secret truth
the key content can't be said,
the last matter couldn't be told
as words lacked availability.

The grief, more painful than death
that invincible sorrowing of *khandab* forest
the illusory circle filled with mist, in self-praise
and voluntary exile, one has to leave alone
siding with the blamed fate
until the last words are
spoken out.

Until revelation of the last matter
one has to leave
amid the indescribable silence
of the spider web, so long breath persists
both body and mind are there, in every tissue
lust and desire, disease and ache
hope and anticipation
and in the invisible world
the endless hide and seek of life and death.

Twenty three

My fate, most unfortunate
is beyond capacity for a sinless life
both statement and sentence
incomprehensible
darkness, seamless
is the full resting place
time and again
the infringement of truth
without one's knowledge
the result of previous birth
is my due, my right always,
I am empty and voiceless
in a dislocated dwelling.

Is it the warning of a
great catastrophe or the
over all vision of merger
or the wailing of human race
fall or the ultimate extinct
of the pattern of a moral life?
No reply from the opposites.
the long manifesto of silence
in the mouth hole of gray death
the imaginative heaven
is both small and scarce.

Life, hackneyed
the deeper anguish of irregular,
inexpressible and disarrayed,
time, chilled
the world of pale and bluish

feeling a barricaded prison
great bluish repression
spectacular night of the sky
unstirred, deeper and long.

Was it misfortune to arrive
at this inauspicious moment?
If affliction was inevitable
it should have come
while I was unknown and
unfamiliar, while the first
step out of mother's womb
to touch the earth.
But what a misfortune do I have?
While shaking with
delirious overwhelmingness
to care of the survival
of a committed life
was misfortune ever to reach?

Twenty four

Where is the incentive to cross over ?
Where is a friend so selfless to assist
in adversity?
Where is pure love?
Perhaps never to avail any of us
during this life.

Where is the scope to redeem oneself
from the eternal sorrow?
Wherever one gazes
grief, pitch dark
floating bridges like
unrealistic ambitions in between;
distress, indescribable, cruel joke
in memorable days
life accursed, still exalted
in grief, happiness and amorous love.

The futile misapplication of
complex words, the unconquerable
mind-boggling, moral revolt
in the cold war of anarchy
fall of rhyme, inevitable'
the large-heartedness of belief and ideal
extinct totally, disjointed compulsion
compassionate, bated breath,
the lucrative life's remnants
at the middle point of
enjoyment and sacrifice.

Life, whatever transgression be it
is lovable for me, I am committed to it,
this is my decision, soulful.

Like the crying long breath
of a dull candle, life stands
before the honeyed grove of time
in the momentary soundless
love making, illusory snare
of guilefulness
integrity and ideologue
are eroded both.

Whether it is the unuttered blessing
of a deity or irresistible curse
this one
under whose command, I am repeatedly
misfired perplexed and motionless
still my mind bird, perched on the
bough of misfortune dreams
of a different world
where the sky and the earth
embrace each other
in the uncommon
supreme consciousness.

My perpetual indifferent mind
is infatuated by the enticement
of the world of dead
overwhelmed by the possibility
of mirth and affluence, frigid by the
firmness of grief
one and all in shape and meaning.

This world of expiration
is like the flickering lamp, deepened
in abject mystery,
at other time
a special unit of fulfilment.

Twenty five

If at all death has to arrive
let it come in a plain simpler way like
a loyal friend with a soundless rhyme.
In every passing there is the beginning
of a new being. Like life every death is sweet
and attractive, an integral part of the same.

In every death, the old face hides within
the new face begins to smile,
new leaves spring up from the bare tree
the visible world is tinged by
greenishness, life metamorphoses
into an incomparable garden.

That when a new life takes birth
cutting across the bloody veins,
the dry leaves would fall from the
bare tree, the rush of new leaves
would sparkle everywhere,
amid tumult and commotion,
a great unknown world shall born
tearing apart the womb of darkness.

The disobedient mind, prompt, is allured
with the sweet love of attraction
busy always with the events, non-existent
darkened, rotates Kalachakra,
anger bursts out, grief tiresome, unmoved
in the rigid sphere of imminent death
the mind is restive and drenched with sorrow
but swift with delicate love and heart string.

Is death a great feeling
for the living beings of thousand ages?
Is it an easy medium to understand this
and the after world. Death, the holy powder
of a new advertence, an invisible halo
that touches a life once only
without any
quest or aim.

Twenty six

In every blink, like the dark clouds
the faces gloomy, float about.
whose face is that? Is it of my dearest enemy
the delicate heart is paled into the fire of ruins,
like an assured fate line
the map is clear and distinct
the fate, inevitable is invincible.

For the ritual of a mortal body
all social laws, rules are meaningless,
the unconditional benediction of
euthanasia and delicate coexistence.

I am the mute witness
of all the events happening around,
there is no way than
witness them silently
within me and outside
ache all along
the tempered obstinacy
is burnt to ashes
by the fire of humiliation
day by day
saturated with anger.

In the war against life
it is not unique
to win or defeat
in order to win
one has to suffer defeat at times
before small people

one has to get away forcibly from
one's own destiny, strength
being terrified one has to find out clue
to one's self defence
in a desolate mood.

At each moment
I feel as if like a stray dog
I am born to be wounded,
my amenable glow,
the great of creativity
the artistic expression
everything futile and meaningless.

Twenty seven

In my hand, the lethal pot
in every limb, the bluish torture
the sun of hope is declined
westerly, still I have
enough faith in my integrity.

In order to cherish selfish ends
there is no remorse if the lexicon
of justice changes its course
thousand times, whatever has to
would happen, no strength to protest
this life, in a way to survive
would stop accidentally
in between, may dash against
but no where to run off.

In every moment, I feel
as if I am born to withstand
slings and arrows of the whole world,
I exist like a scattered unwanted plant
with a little quiver under the stirred water
a life bleary like an extinguished flame.
under the coverage of skin
there is sea of
irremediable disease fretful and vexatious
and my sorrow exceeds limit
day by day.

In which unprecedented event
my life smothers like an illusory
reflection dazzles in the ruined tree

in a yogic posture, I console myself
at every moment that this world
life's funerary
the daily pilgrim of
enjoyment and dispassion
the life universe
is bracketed with
life and death.

Twenty eight

One day or other
life would question
in a simpler way
in an unprepared moment
on the invisible stage
there would be play of chess
entailing upon treachery,
in the hope of appropriating
something.

The simple answers of all questions
don't come to me in time,
the mind, an integrated orchard of
acquiescence and dissent
our destiny has paved over the way with us
the question doesn't come
how to exercise one's right
on the other.

The dearest friend and beloved
loving mother
kin of filial bond,
one can't exercise one's right
on any one, leave alone the
ill fate or the blind invisible destiny.

I am the fledgling
unable to find my way
amid the rush of yawning sounds,
I am myself a sound, a part too,
my conscience, a captive

an abounding feeling,
dedicated intellectual honesty,
ideological integrity and the phlegmatic body
is exhausted by the
compulsive disconnectedness.

There is no escape
from the great sorrow
no respite from the terrible mistake
no spontaneous purity in thought
no end to moral destitution or escape
no salvation, where is that universal,
perennial and integral force of liberty,
symbol of love
that stands well known
all over the world.

Twenty nine

In the turning point of history
I am so tired and overthrown
that I have no time to brood over
birth and beyond, not aware of the
exit point from enmeshment
of the tragic life. The corrupt, loose
departmental minister and
the egoist, immoral secretary have
no end to their deceptiveness, nothing in my hand
to get rid of ailment, anything happens
there is nothing of my wish
to have direct bearing on it.

In each of my limb there is bluish pain
life proceeds apace through sweet love
I feel as if at each moment, I am born to tear me apart,
I would remain incomprehensible
like an obscure poem
and this be my fate.

Each path that leads to compromise
gets closed one by one
in every moment, my experienced
come across the omen
how long I would contemplate on the
enchanting *mantra* of tragedy
and failure in this mortal world,
how longwearing the wreath of hibiscus
I would look silently at the air, sun, moon,
Indra, Varuna
and all the deities as witnesses

would burn severely in the life jagna
wearing the costume of ghee and
lying on the mattress
of fire how long, how
long?

I am yet to die
Due to the earned strength of virtue,
Unable to convince me if the blessing of
euthanasia is my determined fate.
For no reason , my life span
gets lengthened day by day
and I mourn at every moment
of this life.

I am in true sense
an unfortunate incarnation
of Bishadayoga.

Thirty

What do I feel like this at times?
Without any reason, I start being
afraid of my own shadow, nothing
is driven by avarice, understand nothing
why the mind becomes unbridled
don't feel like calling the clay world
that secures me
as of my own.

Like a delicate moringa blown over in the storm
I may crumble into the ground but won't
bend down, may fall like the heavy rain drop of
first Asadha
in extreme silence but never to
surrender my strength,
existence
without any condition.

For long I have felt
the experience of fatal blow
on my limbs
I know in my absence
A new life would emerge
from the burnt ashes
pushing out the cursed womb
its bloody sinews
new leaves would sprout
untimely from the denuded tree,
again the sweet smell of leaves, buds
and flowers would run across the surrounding
area, the exalted air would rise about

playing music of sahnai against wings of the storm
and the blue sky turn deep blue.
Various species of butterflies
and dark bees of deep hue play tunes
with waves of song, a new life springs up
tearing apart
the blue sinews, womb
and the unbruised cunt would keep the small
delicate feet
on the ground.

Thirty one

I know doubly,
there is no alternative
to lakhs of cry, no definite answers to
all eternal queries
I am aware of my failure, futility
sweet frail love, mysterious void
and the unspoken uncertainty, meaningless.
I know… know them.

Filled with overwhelming repetition,
in each branch of the life tree, quiet and delicate
the cursed bird chatters daily whose golden wings
carry strength to fly away
but the deity's evil eye
makes the wings clipped at once,
The sky and the storm are cloven
the sculpted orchard of paradox,
the whole life rigorous
both fate and destiny
are firm sure.

My unseen as has raised me
I have to live in
the curse or blessing
of God wouldn't turn failure
I have my helpless extant in
between seen and virtue
my destiny can't be surpassed.

How tired, weak this helpless man is?
his infatuated mind, irresistible

accumulated languor, mind shaky
wondrous birth episode
even though he knows it well
his journey path from the auspicious
moment of his birth
is indefinite, endless.

Even after termination of the mortal body,
there is no end to this journey, the beginning too
the mortal being goes beyond life and death
man, himself is his creator and saboteur
the beginning of the beginning
ending of the end
in the world of death
this being sure and certain.

Thirty two

For whom this mourning
whose creation or decay,
in defeat, who is dearer to whom,
vanquished who? Is anyone an enemy
or friend since birth?

No simple answers for such questions,
each interrogation can't rise up to its standard
I am firm in my own faith
I am, my own inquisitive
and reply thereof.

I am a mute witness
to the evanescent century,
a lonely traveller of an eternal exile
the holy chanted hymn of *veda*
coming out of the forest,
even if waiting for a birth
I won't bend down like the
flexible pair of canes,
I have to leave alone'
eternally for a gleam of light,
a moment of happiness.

What an ill-fated I am!
Have no clue to get along the rest part of
life, whenever floating against
the current, no one to rescue
tears unabated, drop down from the eyes
the hand of time, invisible stretches at me
like a dark shadow, how long

should I smother in a fiery inferno
by the ill effects of the planet, in the ruinous
world of life, time and again would
be an affront to me without rationale,
brooding over injustice, the entire limbs are
bruised by the ill-famed thorny crown
my virility, egoist still doesn't
succumb to the fate or God either.

Thirty three

It is my misfortune that
All mishaps happen before my eyes.
Ill luck, a terrible shadow alike follows me
I am helpless like a frightened suffering,
devoid of wit and knowledge
the defaced masks of brothers
in *kapatapasa* (trickery chess)
turn all hopes to pale and thin.

They stifle in the fire of envy
to meet selfish ends,
like blind Dhritarastra
struggle tenaciously to ransack
the lotus grove of the dreamy poet
those are sky and the earth
know not the calm , immaculate and honeyed sky
of the poet, his writing an uncommon
creative halo,
the vibrational *pasupata of* ruin and holocaust
sabdabrahma of the poet, the brightened jasmine
of Nandan forest, the poet himself a *tandav* of words
stands like a mad gambler.

I have utmost faith in my own writing
calm, motionless,
joyous straddling a fatal wound,
like the sky of a threefold evening
friendless even in hard times.

Out of silence, indifferent
quiet numbness

an embryo would take birth
and on whose great blow
the treacherous sweet grove
of conspirators would fall into pieces,
also the magnificent building
made out of the conspiracy of the
frenzied ruler.

Thirty four

The pathway of this world is
flooded with mortality
timely and untimely
filled with tales of missteps.
There, death is an attractive handwriting
of beauty, the eligible heir of life.

Like the setting sun
behind the siju forest
beyond the hill, I am a captive
in the *madhusala* of an earnest life
empty is my life pot,
the great stupid world
devoid of prosperity
is like a recent widow,
I am just a wayfarer
of the inn, perplexed and dutiless.

I am helpless
like a bald tree on a rocky mound
as if a saffron saint
no shade or light
action or reaction,
what is good or bad,
pride or prestige
anger or entreat to me,
what of that
the blessing of victory
or the curse of defeat,
I bathe my body intermittently
in the blood of Ganga

I am that berserk proud Duryodhana
of the condemned century.

In every route of
agreement, hangs the cruel plate
of forbiddingness, path thorny
evanescent time, freezes eye of the
seasoned the cataract of illusion
the dove of peace is wounded
by an arrow of the archer, bloodied
and now the remnant of death.

Every day and night
I die and take birth
thousand times
wear out repeatedly
by the four walls of failures
I genuflect before the
fate, accept it singularly for this life.

Thirty five

One day or other
may be good or bad
tiding over the diplomatic pretence
the seven warriors would face their end
by the armour of words.

Each word, elegant and sharp
in a mundane circle, has its unique look,
incomparable charm
like the dazzle of a star
shrouded in mystery,
words full of brilliance
in this mundane world.

For years together
I used to survive in this mortal earth,
unrecognised, the sorrowing feel of
forty four years
has taught me this life
a pedestrian move
I am here today
But don't know where would be tomorrow.
So many secret pains of
Skylab are falling in pieces
on me, the world ever saturated
with death.
Death would come
like a v.i.p, so with sandal paste and fragrance
all over the body,
I sit with readiness
Like a bridegroom.

Defeat in victory
victory in defeat
are my written fate.
I am not in control of happiness
or a slave to sorrow
my mind and heart are like
a mourning house
wherein the west wind
blows constantly.

My destiny is but an obscure raining sky
future mysterious, in its
inevitable innate wish
there is deep imprint
of the sudden death line
in the blue body
the fancy towel of dignity
in every particle golden talisman
of pledges, the great utterance
of silent decision,
the austere unbearable
and implacable worries.

Thirty six

In my bewail and tear
lies the new consciousness
of Bibhuti. All mundane anguish of
the honeyed life is enveloped
with broken wings.
The doubtful life is disconsolate
from fear and helplessness,
the three worlds quiver with
demoniac rejoicing.
At once the sin of jungle
spreads about its beauty.

A great suffering
within the sin of forest ,
the social life is shaken and tormented with
uncertainty, the atrocious calling of
extant and extinct, the ray of hope is
feeble before the blind and unforeseen rule,
the possibility of the ampleness
of joy is meagre.
At the crossroads of history
the fortune afflicted is
like the stagnant water, the bestial life
is undisciplined without love
and futile application of words
the loyal mind is shivered
with adversity, inexperienced,
future blind and uncertain.

Thirty seven

Come. Oh! Revered guest
Like the torrential rain of
Sravana, the wet month,
The cumulus deluge in the scowl, rhyme
of storm in the agile feet, drowned with
devastating dance of tandav
and getting no way out of the mirage of ego
drunk by the dazzle of manliness
you come to my
competitive picturesque courtyard
would advance a couple of steps
further to garland you, console with
the offer of love without any fear.
You are the inevitable good luck
of future, a feeling of boundless silence.
You are the intrepid talisman
of cheerful bliss,
filled with the tales of inefficiency.

Your unwounded melody
is embellished with the tune of *meghamalhara*,
cloud beat, your ever raining compassion
would spill like milk from the clay pot
to overflow with each consciousness,
an unknown joy shivers with the urban tendon
Oh! Revered gentle guest
you are the attractive handwriting of beauty
for a number of births.

Thirty eight

The time of your arrival
when knocks at the door,
time at once slips away from the hand
like a wanton lover
the ultimate drop of oblation
falls on the
altar of desire.
The five senses
turn ice
the kite of air accidently unweaves
yarn of the shuttle
to hide in the blueness of the sky,
the vigorous body of flesh and blood
turns inert, the deformed gruesome
scenes of near future
dance like ghosts before the eyes
the man lying his head
in the lap of death, raises his ears
for the calmly stepping, soundless.

The man , searching himself in
silence of the space
flees away from him,
gives ear to his own stepping
just then, a clay man, a new arrival
dashes at once like a meteor
from an invisible world, a planet
undiscovered and touches me
with a delicate love.
Questions me again smilingly:
'you the pedestrian

to which court palace
you do travel,
which inaccessible Anandalok
you move ahead,
What is your sorrow after all?
Like Shyama, poised you are
both in life and death'
I look at him with unblinking eyes
Up to my feel and for a definite incident
I feel it useless to mourn
and keep myself quiet therefore and
in the scene
the juicy words become mysterious.

Black Eagle Books

www.blackeaglebooks.org
info@blackeaglebooks.org

Black Eagle Books, an independent publisher, was founded as a nonprofit organization in April, 2019. It is our mission to connect and engage the Indian diaspora and the world at large with the best of works of world literature published on a collaborative platform, with special emphasis on foregrounding Contemporary Classics and New Writing.

www.ingramcontent.com/pod-product-compliance
Lightning Source LLC
Chambersburg PA
CBHW020545080526
44583CB00013B/997